C000018073

1 MONTH OF
FREE
READING

at
www.ForgottenBooks.com

By purchasing this book you are eligible for one month membership to ForgottenBooks.com, giving you unlimited access to our entire collection of over 1,000,000 titles via our web site and mobile apps.

To claim your free month visit:
www.forgottenbooks.com/free1297526

ISBN 978-0-428-94826-9
PIBN 11297526

Historic, Archive Document

Do not assume content reflects current
scientific knowledge, policies, or practices.

Ponderosa Pine-Bunchgrass Ranges in the Central Rocky Mountains:

The Status of Our Knowledge

O. Currie

USDA Forest Service
Research Paper RM-159
Rocky Mountain Forest and
Range Experiment Station
Forest Service
U.S. Department of Agriculture
Fort Collins, Colorado 80521

December 1975

Abstract

Currie, Pat O.
   1975. Grazing management of ponderosa pine-bunchgrass ranges of the central Rocky Mountains: The status of our knowledge. USDA For. Serv. Res. Pap. RM-159, 24 p. Rocky Mt. For. and Range Exp. Stn., Fort Collins, Colo. 80521

   Pine-bunchgrass ranges have historically been important livestock-producing areas in the central Rocky Mountains. Grazing will continue to be important, but in conjunction with other uses of the land. Livestock-management techniques are well developed and soundly based on research within the pine-bunchgrass type. There is a need, however, to understand the interrelationships of other land uses, particularly as they relate to human population pressures. Research needs, as well as what is known, are described for several vegetation cover types. Other resources, such as timber, soil, and water, are evaluated in relation to grazing.

Keywords: Grazing management, pine-bunchgrass type, *Pinus ponderosa*.

GRAZING MANAGEMENT OF PONDEROSA PINE-BUNCHGRASS RANGES OF THE CENTRAL ROCKY MOUNTAINS:
The Status of Our Knowledge

Pat O. Currie, Principal Range Scientist
Rocky Mountain Forest and Range Experiment Station[1]

[1] Central headquarters maintained at Fort Collins, in cooperation with Colorado State University.

Contents

                                                                    Page

Physiographic Features 1

    Geology 3

    Soils 3

    Climatic Characteristics 4

Vegetation 5

Early Grazing Use and Direction for Research 7

Plant and Animal Management on Native Ranges 8

Establishment and Management of Seeded Ranges 12

    Adaptability and Seeding Methods 12

    Grazing Management 14

Cultural Manipulation and Integrated Systems of Management 16

    Cultural Practices 16

    Integrating Native-Seeded Ranges 17

    Additional Practices 18

Factors Affecting the Future of Livestock Grazing and Range Research 19

    Land Use Patterns and Priorities 19

    Relating Demands to Resource Capabilities 20

Literature Cited 21

Common and Scientific Names of Plants and Animals 23

GRAZING MANAGEMENT OF PONDEROSA

PINE-BUNCHGRASS RANGES OF THE CENTRAL

ROCKY MOUNTAINS:

The Status of Our Knowledge

Pat O. Currie

Historically, ponderosa pine-bunchgrass[2] ranges have been important livestock-producing areas in the central Rocky Mountains. Beginning with the discovery of gold in Colorado in 1858, exploitation of the timber resource has been common throughout most of the pine type, and nearly all commercial stands have been harvested one to several times. Harvesting this timber resource altered the vegetation complex by enlarging the natural openings, or creating new ones. Homesteaders then established farms and livestock grazing operations to feed themselves and the rudimentary mining and settlement communities. Thousands of acres were plowed and planted to small grains, hay, and hardy row crops.

The forage resources were heavily utilized by livestock. Hay crops for cattle, horses, and mules were in high demand. The cattle industry expanded most rapidly between 1880 and 1890. Sheep grazing, however, did not assume any importance until World War I, and then only small numbers occupied ponderosa pine ranges. By the mid-1930's animal months of grazing finally began to decline on National Forest lands. Early reductions came slowly, but today less than one-third of peak numbers are grazing on National Forest lands in Colorado. Similar use patterns developed on the pine lands of New Mexico and Wyoming. In the whole central Rocky Mountain area, long-overdue recognition of the adverse effects of mismanagement on watersheds was

[2]*Common and scientific names of plants and animals mentioned are listed at the end of the Paper.*

an important factor responsible for reductions in grazing pressure.

The purpose of this Paper is to bring together what we have learned about grazing these lands, the relationship of this grazing to other uses, and identify the needs for further knowledge.

Physiographic Features

The ponderosa pine-bunchgrass type can best be described as a zone of the central Rockies encompassing about 17 million acres in Wyoming, Colorado, and New Mexico (fig. 1). Only two small islands of the vegetation type occur in Wyoming, along the North Platte drainage. Approximately 10 million acres are in Colorado on both sides of the Continental Divide along watercourses of the South Platte, Arkansas, and Colorado Rivers. The remaining acreages in New Mexico are primarily along drainages of the Rio Grande and Pecos Rivers. The total zone varies from 5 to 25 miles in width and ranges from 5,000 to 9,500 feet in elevation over the 400-mile north-to-south distance. Almost all of the pine-bunchgrass grazing lands of the three States are within this well-defined zone.

Topography of the pine-bunchgrass type is rough and dissected by many tributaries of the major rivers, which often head well above the type. This dissection contributes to a great diversity of landscape aspects (fig. 2) which, combined with the base geology, exerts a profound influence on the vegetation and soils of the type.

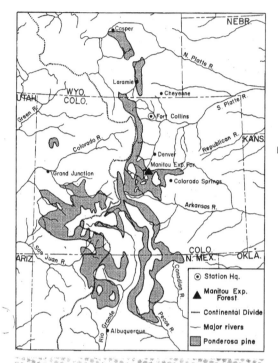

Figure 1.—Distribution of ponderosa pine in the central Rocky Mountains.

Figure 2.—Dissection of the topography creates a diversity of landscape aspects, which contributes to a mosaic of vegetation patterns.

Of the four common soils, soils derived from granite are the most abundant in the pine type, and may or may not have clay subsoils. Those without a clay layer have a gravelly, sandy loam surface soil, 4 to 8 inches thick, which grades into the parent rock. The parent rock may be weathered and crumbly, or unweathered and massive. Soils on south slopes are drier and contain less surface litter and organic matter than those on north slopes. Where litter or plant cover is absent, the surface is protected by a gravel pavement over a layer of fine-textured material.

Less abundant are granitic soils with clay subsoils. These soils may be residual, or may have developed on old alluvial terraces consisting of granitic materials. Surface soils are 8 to 10 inches thick and are frequently underlain by red clay subsoils that may be 2 or more feet deep. The clay subsoil is compact and well cemented when dry, and lime deposits are occasionally found on small gravels at the base of the subsoil. The granitic parent material is often decomposed, and consists of a reddish brown gravel. A gravel pavement develops where the soil surface is devoid of litter or plant cover. Both of the granitic types of soils are very susceptible to erosion.

Soils developed from schist have a fine, sandy loam surface layer that varies in depth up to 20 inches. Surface soil grades into the parent rock; subsoils are generally absent. The parent rock is often weathered and cracked, which facilitates the movement of water into the substrata. Soils on south aspects are drier than those on the north, and contain less surface litter and organic matter.

Characteristics of soils developed from shales depend upon the aspect and kind of plant cover present. Soils on south aspects are shallow, with surface soils ranging from 6 to 12 inches thick, while those on north aspects or those covered with a dense stand of pine, oak brush, or grass have surface soils 8 to 18 inches thick. Blocklike subsurface soils of varying thickness and predominately clay in texture grade into the parent material. Soils from both aspects are fertile, but are subject to excessive sheet erosion when devoid of an adequate plant cover. Unlike the granitic soils, internal drainage is slow and moisture retention is high.

Associated with the major soils are alluvial soils which develop in valley bottoms and upland pockets formed behind rock outcrops. These alluvial soils are generally deep, and have only surface soils 6 to 18 inches thick. They are brown to dark brown in color, of varying textures, neutral in reaction, and grade into the parent alluvial material which is often loose and porous. These soils have considerable moisture storage capacity, but are easily eroded once gullies start in the valleys.

Climatic Characteristics

Climate in the zone ranges from semiarid to sub-humid, with average rainfall varying from about 15 or 16 inches in New Mexico and south-central Colorado to over 25 inches in the Medicine Bow Range of Wyoming. Altitudinal range of the ponderosa pine type differs between the Eastern and Western Slopes of the Continental Divide (fig. 3).

The distribution and form of precipitation, which are extremely important to plant growth, also vary on each side of the Divide. On the Western Slope, annual precipitation averages 14 to 18 inches in the pine type. About half of this precipitation comes as snow through the fall and winter months, and half as rain between April and September. June tends to be rather dry. The severely cold, Arctic air masses that frequently dominate the Eastern Slope, and particularly the Central Plains, only occasionally influence temperatures on the Western Slope. Thus minimum temperatures are more moderate. Otherwise, temperatures are rather comparable for the two ponderosa pine areas.

On the Eastern Slope, daily temperatures range from an average maximum of about 50°F in January and February to approximately 85°F in July and August. Seldom do daytime temperatures exceed 90°F. These same months have the lowest and highest minimum daily temperatures, which average about -10°F in the winter to about 35°F in the summer. The growing season is rather short, about 125 days. Extreme cold from Arctic air is not uncommon, and temperatures may drop to -40 to -50°F for short periods.

Precipitation on the Eastern Slope generally ranges between 12 and 20 inches. The summary of 30 years' precipitation (fig. 4) for the Manitou Experimental Forest, Colorado, is characteristic of that for the Eastern Slope pine type. Commonly, two-thirds or more of the annual precipitation is received during the period from April through September, with July and August being the wettest months.

On both sides of the Continental Divide, the number of clear days averages 100-140 (Reifsnyder and Lull 1965). The average number of cloudy days averages between 80 and 120. The remainder are

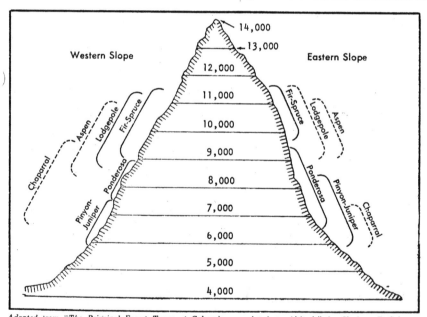

Adapted from "The Principal Forest Types of Colorado as related to Altitude" by Herbert E. Schwan.

Figure 3.—The principal forest types of Colorado as related to altitude; broken lines indicate subclimaxes (from Miller and Choate 1964).

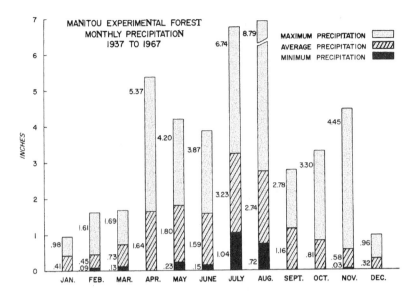

Figure 4.—Summary of monthly precipitation data, Manitou Experimental Forest, 1937 to 1967.

partly cloudy days brought about by the summer rainfall patterns characteristic of the pine type. Storms are a result of mass air disturbances initiated by early morning heating. When these local warm convection currents rise and meet the cool air coming from the higher mountains, severe thunderstorms may result. With the exception of these cloudburst storms, which produce large amounts of rainfall in short periods, the climate in the ponderosa pine zone is more moderate than on the adjacent Central Plains.

Vegetation

The pine-bunchgrass type of the central Rocky Mountains is a complex of plant communities. Its one apparent and common characteristic, however, is that of open grassland parks interspersed among forested areas (fig. 5). On north slopes at high elevations in the western portion of the ponderosa pine-bunchgrass type there is a gradual mergence with the spruce-fir type, or with the lodgepole pine

Figure 5.—The ponderosa pine-bunchgrass type is characterized by open grasslands interspersed within the tree community. On the higher ridges and north slopes (background), ponderosa pine merges with the spruce-fir or lodgepole pine types.

type described by Alexander (1974). Along the eastern margin, a series of north-south hogbacks and foothills are covered with a mixture of ponderosa pine, mountain brush, and native grasses. In the southern portion, the eastern areas support stands of pinyon-juniper that intergrade with ponderosa pine as the land slopes upward to the west.

Ponderosa pine-bunchgrass ranges include four vegetation subtypes of special interest. The largest subtype productive for grazing consists of open stands of timber with an extensive herbaceous understory (fig. 6). In the northern part of the type, Idaho fescue is prominent, but is replaced by Arizona fescue to the south. Mountain muhly, blue grama, Parry oatgrass, sedges, and a variety of forbs are common throughout the type. These same species comprise the vegetation of the open grassland parks, but usually in much more dense stands. The open parks along watercourses give way to meadows and streambanks covered with sedges, rushes, hairgrasses, wheatgrasses, and willows. The fourth subtype is composed of closed stands of ponderosa pine with almost no understory, but with a litter mat of needles and small twigs, or at higher elevations or on north exposures, mixtures of pine and Douglas-fir. Grass cover varies in density from lush meadows to an extremely thin and patchy cover on steep, unstable, south-facing slopes.

In the southern half of the ponderosa pine type, oak brush has invaded cutover pine stands. In many places the oak brush is of sufficient density to be classified as a separate type. As a result of past fires or other disturbances, quaking aspen mixed with ponderosa pine sometimes occupies large acreages very productive for grazing (fig. 7). In New Mexico, shrubby cinquefoil is also abundant on depleted sites within the pine type. These areas generally have a low potential for grazing unless the species composition is improved.

As many as 35 species of grasses are present on ponderosa pine ranges in good to excellent condition (Johnson and Reid 1958). Forbs are also numerous but fluctuate from year to year, with only a few species frequent or abundant enough to warrant consideration. On average pine-bunchgrass ranges, generally only six forage species — little bluestem, blue grama, Arizona fescue, mountain muhly, sun sedge, and fringed sagebrush — make up about 95 percent of the herbage composition by weight.

Costello and Schwan (1946) considered each of the plant communities in the pine type to be a transitional stage between bare ground and the ultimate pine or fir climax forest (fig. 8). Of particular interest from the grazing standpoint, however, are the intermediate stages of any one of a hundred or more communities that are influenced by such things as livestock use, timber management activities, fire, base geology, soil type, and other influences.

Generally, range managers have attempted to retain or achieve the fescue-mountain muhly sub-

Figure 6.—Open stands of ponderosa pine occupied by good stands of the dominant grasses and forbs constitute the largest subtype productive for livestock grazing.

Figure 7.—Quaking aspen mixed with ponderosa pine forms large communities throughout the pine type.

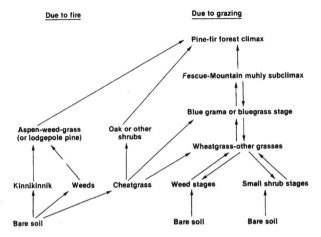

Figure 8.—Some common secondary successions in the ponderosa pine zone (from Costello and Schwan 1946).

climax. This stage is characterized by an abundance of Arizona fescue and mountain muhly in the southern two-thirds of the zone. Idaho fescue usually replaces the Arizona fescue toward the northern border of Colorado and into Wyoming. At the upper limit of the pine zone, Thurber fescue will replace Arizona fescue, and it may be associated with the Idaho fescue. In the Southwest, this association may have substantial amounts of sheep fescue.

In addition to the fescues and mountain muhly, other desirable grasses are Parry oatgrass, June-grass, and little bluestem. Those of lesser importance include blue grama, western wheatgrass, slender wheatgrass, and bottlebrush squirreltail. Other less desirable grasses are sleepygrass, pullup muhly, and tumblegrass.

Among the less transient and usually conspicuous forbs are Fremont and Parry geraniums, purple milkvetch, western yarrow, Lambert loco, cinque-foils, asters, and bluebells. Less common forbs which are usually present but not abundant if ranges have been well taken care of include: hairy goldaster, trailing fleabane, and fringed sagebrush.

Early Grazing Use and Direction for Research

The bulk of grazing management research in the ponderosa pine-bunchgrass type of the central Rockies has been done at the Manitou Experimental Forest, 28 miles northwest of Colorado Springs. Most of the virgin ponderosa pine on the Experimental Forest was cut over between 1880 and 1885. Some of the cutover and natural openings were plowed and cultivated in the late 1800's and early 1900's. Between 1912 and 1933, from 225 to more than 300 head of cattle and horses grazed these lands. The use period was quite long, May 1-December 15, and generally heavy. This heavy use — and sometimes abuse — which disturbed or removed the plant cover, in combination with the inherent high erosion hazards of the granitic soils in the pine type, prompted early research to be directed toward erosion-related problems. Thus, early grazing management research was directed toward the broader aspects of proper management and grazing as it related to watershed problems.

Several grazing studies were started when the Manitou Experimental Forest was established in 1937. One of the first problems evaluated was that of surface runoff and erosion (Dunford 1954). Six 1/100-acre plots were measured in the bunchgrass type over a period of approximately 20 years. The plots were distributed in two batteries of three each, lying on a 17-percent north-facing slope. Vegetation was primarily grasses, dominated by Arizona fescue and mountain muhly. The relatively permeable soil originated from gravelly alluvium and outwash of Pikes Peak granite.

Following a 4-year calibration period, cattle grazing treatments were initiated in 1941. Two plots were grazed heavily, two moderately, and two were left ungrazed as controls (fig. 9). Pretreatment calibrations had estimated that runoff was substantially the same, 0.24 to 0.27 inch per season, on all plots during the summer rainfall period. In 12 years of grazing, moderately grazed plots average 0.22 inch of runoff per season and heavily grazed averaged 0.34 inch per season. Nongrazed plots averaged 0.11 inch per season. This was equivalent to the surface runoff and soil losses shown in figure 10.

Erosion occurred almost exclusively during the months of July and August. During calibration, average erosion for the summer period varied from 111 to 163 pounds per acre. After grazing treatment, annual soil loss from moderate grazing averaged 145 pounds per acre for 13 rainstorms, heavy use 316 pounds, and nonuse 134 pounds per acre.

Vegetation on the moderately grazed plots of this study (Dunford 1954) was quite comparable to that on range described as being in good condition by Reid and Love (1951) for the Elk Ridge area on the Roosevelt National Forest. Infiltration rates on plots in good condition were 118 percent greater than on plots in very poor condition, 80 percent greater than those in poor, and 35 percent greater than for plots in fair condition. Also, erosion rates from plots in good condition were about one-fourth those from plots in very poor condition, and one-half those in fair condition.

In the same study, Reid and Love (1951) analyzed principal uses and values of the area, including surveys to determine forage condition and trend in the vegetation complex. They concluded that range improvement would have little overall effect on watershed conditions because the principal areas utilized by cattle were grassland types which occupy only a small part of the total watershed. They further concluded that tree overstory, rather than grazing, was the most important factor in reducing runoff and erosion, particularly on south exposures.

From this work in reference to watershed protection, it was concluded that a moderate rate of grazing is not detrimental. On the flat open areas or gentle slopes where cattle usually graze, removing about 35 percent of the current growth will not adversely affect the watersheds. Heavy grazing, where about 50 percent or more of the herbage is removed, will subject the soils of the pine type to an accelerated erosion rate considered to be above normal.

Plant and Animal Management on Native Ranges

Other early studies were devoted to determining optimum grazing intensities for maintenance of plant cover and beef production on native ranges. Johnson (1953) summarized the results of these intensity-of-use investigations from 1941 through 1947. Smith (1967) incorporated later and more comprehensive data into a bulletin on how ponderosa pine-bunchgrass ranges should be grazed. It included discussions of effect of grazing intensity on plant growth, cattle gains, and soil responses, and relation of grazing intensity to income.

Herbage yields and associated stocking rates are extremely variable on ponderosa pine-bunchgrass ranges. The yields of grass and sedge herbage varies from about 50 to 75 pounds per acre under dense timber to approximately 1,200 pounds per acre on moderately stocked open grasslands (fig. 11). Grass-

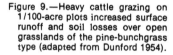

Figure 9.—Heavy cattle grazing on 1/100-acre plots increased surface runoff and soil losses over open grasslands of the pine-bunchgrass type (adapted from Dunford 1954).

Grazing Results In — RUNOFF   SOIL LOSS

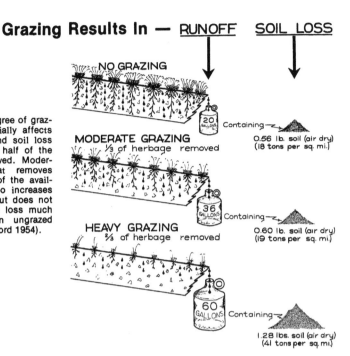

Figure 10.—The degree of grazing use substantially affects surface runoff and soil loss when more than half of the herbage is removed. Moderate grazing that removes about one-third of the available herbage also increases surface runoff, but does not increase the soil loss much above that from ungrazed range (from Dunford 1954).

lands protected from grazing produce yields of up to 1,600 pounds per acre. Smith (1967) reported that, after 17 years of treatment, the annual yields of grasses and sedges were maintained under light or moderate use, but heavy grazing substantially reduced yields. Plant species contributing to these yields were influenced by grazing use. As shown below, the major bunchgrasses were favored by light to moderate grazing, while undesirables increased with heavier use:

Favored by light and moderate grazing	Favored by heavy grazing	Not affected by degree of grazing
Mountain muhly	Tumblegrass	Sun sedge
Arizona fescue	Pussytoes	Fringed
Blue grama	Groundsels	sagebrush
Bottlebrush squirreltail	Goosefoot	
Lupines		
Bearberry		
Arkansas rose		

Degree of livestock use was also closely associated with cover types. Most of the livestock grazing was on abandoned fields or the open grassland parks. Cattle grazed some under the open timber type, but the dense timber type was seldom grazed. Where approximately 35 percent of the range is open grassland, 60 percent is open timber, and 5 percent dense timber, about 3.5 to 4 acres are required to graze a yearling animal for a month. If cows and calves are being grazed, about 10 acres are required per pair. These figures are average stocking rates for ranges in fair condition, and will vary with changes in cover type, grazing season, and climatic variables, particularly rainfall.

Stocking rates also depend on such things as size and age of animals, topography or steepness of slope, range condition, and cover type. Rates may vary from as few as 2 to 3 acres to as many as 8 to 15 acres per animal unit month (AUM), depending on slope, condition, and cover type (Costello and Schwan 1946):

Figure 11.—Herbage yields from pine-bunchgrass ranges vary extremely with cover type. This variability is further modified by degree of grazing use. Moderate grazing provides the largest sustained herbage yields (from Smith 1967).

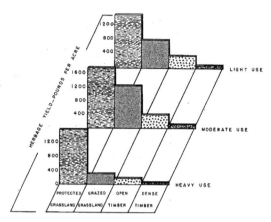

Range condition and percent slope	Acres per AUM
Excellent:	
<20	2-3
20-40	3-4
>40	4-6
Good:	
<20	3-4
20-40	4-6
40-60	6-12
Fair:	
<20	4-8
20-40	6-12
>40	Ordinarily no grazing
Poor:	
<20	8-15
20-40	Ordinarily no grazing
>40	Ordinarily no grazing

Johnson (1953) and Smith (1967) showed that ponderosa pine ranges should be grazed to use 30 to 40 percent of the current annual growth of the major forage grasses to obtain maximum sustained production of both forage and beef. Lighter rates were not harmful to the vegetation, but they were not conducive to a good rate of livestock production. Grazing in excess of 50 percent use of the major grasses resulted in lower livestock production, and harmful, long-lasting damage to the range.

Johnson and Reid (1958) further emphasized that seasonal aspects should be considered in grazing ponderosa pine ranges. Seasonlong summer use was not harmful to pine-bunchgrass ranges, but a range that had a large percent of its forage contributed by Arizona fescue, sedges, or little bluestem would best be used early. Ranges with a predominance of mountain muhly are more suitable for mid- to late-season grazing. These conclusions were based on the observations that Arizona fescue is an early cool-season species, while mountain muhly makes the bulk of its growth late in the season (Smith 1967).

Ponderosa pine-bunchgrass ranges are normally ready for grazing between June 1 and 15, and can be grazed to as late as November 1 to 15. This late fall grazing, however, is not conducive to the best livestock production for yearling animals. After September, animals may frequently lose weight or make almost no gains. The best gains are made early in the grazing season, with a gradual decline each month through September (fig. 12). In general, yearling animals will gain about 1.5 pounds per day in a 5-month season (Smith 1967).

To obtain the 30 to 40 percent recommended use, stubble heights of Arizona fescue plants should average 5 to 6 inches at the end of the grazing season. Mountain muhly will average a 1½- to 2-inch stubble when properly used. At these rates, some plants of each species will remain ungrazed while others will be grazed more than the recommended rate. Other species generally will not need to be considered for determining range condition.

Complementary work on native species by Schuster (1964) showed that root systems of several plants, including the major grasses, were reduced by heavy grazing (table 1). Differences were not significant between moderately grazed and ungrazed plants, however. Root systems of less desirable species such as blue grama and Rocky Mountain pussytoes increased or stayed about the same under heavy grazing.

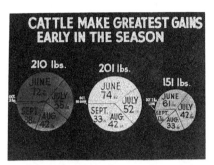

CATTLE MAKE GREATEST GAINS EARLY IN THE SEASON

210 lbs.   201 lbs.   151 lbs.

Figure 12.—Yearling animals make their best weight gain on native ponderosa pine-bunchgrass ranges through the summer months. Gains are good from light or moderate grazing, but decrease appreciably when ranges are used heavily (from Smith 1967).

Infiltration of water and erosion of soil were also related to cattle use of the plant cover. Studies by Love (1953, 1958), Renner and Love (1955), and Dortignac and Love (1960, 1961) showed that infiltration rates remained high or good under moderate grazing, but were poor under a heavy rate of use. They also showed that, if an area is first grazed, and later a portion of the range is excluded from grazing, infiltration increases with time on the excluded areas but not on the grazed areas. Thus the main effect of any degree of cattle grazing was to slow or prevent recovery of water infiltration rates.

Soil losses were much greater on heavily grazed ranges where cattle removed 50 percent or more of the herbage than where 40 percent or less was removed on moderately or lightly grazed ranges (Dunford 1954, Renner and Love 1955, Dortignac and Love 1960). However, even the loss of 400 pounds per acre per inch of runoff on heavily grazed ranges was not considered excessive (Dortignac and Love 1960). Relatively small amounts of soil will be washed from ponderosa pine ranges when erosion rates, as determined by the infiltrometer method, are less than 500 pounds per acre.

Grazing of ponderosa pine-bunchgrass ranges also influences the populations of small mammals.[3] Populations of six rodent species were larger on areas protected from grazing than on adjacent grazed ranges. The **degree** of grazing use did not make any measurable difference in these small mammal populations, however. The rodents preferred either an ungrazed grassland range or an open timber type:

Grassland	**Open timber**
Northern pocket gopher	Deer mouse
Meadow vole	Golden-mantled ground
Thirteen-lined ground	squirrel
squirrel	Colorado chipmunk

Any degree of cattle grazing functioned as a control measure to keep populations lower than on ungrazed areas. Regulation of the height of herbaceous ground cover was evidently the controlling factor in both types.

[3]Reid, Vincent H., Wildlife Biologist, Res. Bur. Sport Fish. and Wildl., USDI Fish and Wildl. Serv., Fort Collins, Colo. (Manuscript in preparation, "Populations of certain rodents on grazed and nongrazed ranges.")

Table 1.—Depth and spread of root systems in relation to grazing of the most common native plants on pine-bunchgrass ranges (from Smith 1967).

Species	Average maximum depth			Average maximum lateral spread[1]		
	No use	Moderate use	Heavy use	No use	Moderate use	Heavy use
	In.	*In.*	*In.*	*In.*	*In.*	*In.*
Arizona fescue..........	44.5	44.1	31.3	12.0	11.3	8.0
Blue grama..............	37.8	42.8	36.0	9.3	7.4	7.1
Fringed sagebrush........	38.2	38.7	26.4	6.4	8.8	6.1
Mountain muhly.........	50.8	44.1	32.1	11.4	8.9	6.8
Rocky Mountain pussytoes	14.0	14.0	19.0	5.0	10.5	5.8

[1]Measured from line projected through plant center.

Establishing and Management of Seeded Ranges

The incorporation of seeded ranges into management systems resulted from extensive early investigations into revegetation practices. For example, during the late 1800's and early 1900's, areas of the pine type were cultivated for a number of years, then abandoned without provision for establishment of vegetative cover (fig. 13). When Johnson (1945) observed secondary successional stages of natural revegetation of abandoned croplands, he concluded that overgrazing could maintain a stand of inferior plants indefinitely. Even with proper management, these ranges were slow to recover, and plow lines associated with characteristic vegetation were readily apparent almost 100 years later. Seeding, however, could restore these areas to a productive condition in a few years (Johnson 1947). Thus, much emphasis on early reseeding work centered largely on planting techniques and species adaptability tests.

On both native and reseeded ranges, the relation of forage removal to soil and vegetation growth received attention before systems-of-grazing experiments were included in research programs. Research on specific relations and responses of individual species are developments of the last few years.

Adaptability and Seeding Methods

Investigations of range reseeding within the ponderosa pine zone have been concentrated largely at the Manitou Experimental Forest. Study of planting techniques and species adaptability were important phases of the early research (fig. 14). Johnson and

Figure 13.—Abandoned fields in the pine type produce only small amounts of low-quality forage. These areas were turned into highly productive cattle ranges by seeding, mainly to introduced grasses or grass-legume mixtures.

Figure 14.—Species adaptability tests were used to establish success ratings for a large number of forage species, varieties, and strains in the pine type (from Hull and Johnson 1955).

Hull (1950) and Hull and Johnson (1955) summarized recommendations of this early research. In addition to the work carried out at Manitou, 14 experimental areas and 391 range seedings were observed throughout the ponderosa pine type. This study resulted in many basic suggestions concerning where, when, what, and how to seed (McGinnies et al. 1963). Another valuable contribution was the development of establishment success ratings for 121 forage species, varieties, and strains. Ratings for the most promising species tested are summarized in table 2 (Hull and Johnson 1955).

Open parks in the pine type have the best economic potential for improvement by seeding, particularly if the areas have been abused and are supporting plants of low to medium quality for grazing. Such areas are characterized by an abundance of species such as sleepygrass, blue grama, trailing fleabane, or fringed sagebrush. Abandoned fields are also particularly suitable for seeding (Johnson and Hull 1950).

Seeding success is closely related to the effort expended in seedbed preparation and elimination of competing vegetation. Excellent stands were commonplace if the best-adapted species were used, and seedbed preparation consisted of moldboard or brushland plowing or using a heavy offset disk (fig.

15). Medium disks or sweeps resulted in good stands. Chisels and field cultivators resulted in only fair to poor stands.

Early-spring and medium- to late-fall plantings gave the best stands in lower elevations of the pine zone. Generally March and early April have enough moisture for seeding in the spring, and fall seeding in October and November is reasonably successful. In the higher part of the zone, both total and higher seasonal moisture permits seeding in April and May on well-prepared seedbeds. September and early October is usually best for fall seeding. In southwestern Colorado and northern New Mexico, seeding in July and August gives good results. Generally, seeding results are more dependable from fall than spring seeding (Hull and Johnson 1955).

Although Sherman big bluegrass appeared to be well adapted and showed promise for grazing in early studies, seedings often failed (McGinnies et al. 1963). Further establishment testing (Currie 1967) showed the species was best established by planting in July or August into a moist seedbed that had been summer fallowed (fig. 16). Controlling the depth of planting to 5/8 inch by means of a double-disk, depth-band drill gave the best results. Roadside stabilization programs with this and other species, seeded in summer, have been successful in the pine type in the Colorado Springs area.

Table 2.—Establishment success rating of species tested on 391 seedings throughout the pine zone of Colorado (from Hull and Johnson 1955).

Species	Times seeded	Seedings by class				
		Excellent	Good	Fair	Poor	Failure
	No.	*No.*	*No.*	*No.*	*No.*	*No.*
Crested wheatgrass	265	64	127	27	21	26
Smooth brome	195	31	88	25	24	27
Yellow sweetclover	153	17	60	26	30	20
Alfalfa	34	4	25		1	4
Timothy	16		8	2	4	2
Intermediate wheatgrass	13	7	5	1		
Orchardgrass	9		3	1	3	2
Western wheatgrass	8	1		3	4	
Kentucky bluegrass	7			1	3	3
Slender wheatgrass	6		1		5	
Alsike clover	5	1	1	1		2
Quackgrass	4	3	1			
Big bluegrass	4	2	1			1
Tall oatgrass	4		2		1	1
Redtop	3		3			
Bulbous bluegrass	3			1	1	1
Russian wildrye	2	1		1		
Blue grama	2				1	1
White clover	2			1		1
Perennial ryegrass	2					2

13

Figure 15.—A variety of equipment was tested and used for seeding establishment in the pine type. Plowing with the brushland plow, cultipacking to firm the seedbed, and planting with a grain drill were used in one operation to minimize costs on suitable areas (from Hull and Johnson 1955).

Figure 16.—Excellent stands of Sherman big bluegrass were obtained by planting into a moist seedbed in July or August. Such stands are characteristic of the potential for abandoned fields in the pine type (from Currie 1967).

Grazing Management

Management studies on reseeded pastures at Manitou Experimental Forest have concentrated on the effects of grazing intensities. Four species — smooth brome, crested wheatgrass, intermediate wheatgrass, and Russian wildrye — and a mixture — smooth brome - crested wheatgrass - yellowblossom sweetclover — were subjected to different intensities of grazing. In 1952, Johnson presented guidelines[4]

[4]Johnson, W. M. Management of reseeded pastures. Paper presented to Colorado Grassland Committee, Jan. 22, 1952.

for grazing reseeded pastures that were based largely on the work conducted at Manitou, followed by a published interim report that summarized the effects of grazing on seeding species (Johnson 1959). A comprehensive final report was published by Currie and Smith (1970).

During 14 years of grazing, a mixture of crested wheatgrass, smooth brome, and yellowblossom sweetclover gave the best sustained forage and live-stock production. The average per-acre weight gain for yearling heifers was highly variable by species and from year to year, however (table 3). This variation was directly related to forage production, which was low in dry years and high in wet years (fig. 17). For example, per-acre gains from the mixture averaged only 12.8 pounds in 1954 when growing-season rainfall was 9.03 inches, but went up to 99.8 pounds per acre in 1957 when rainfall was 15.62 inches. Crested wheatgrass showed a similar trend, with gains being about eight times more in wet years than dry years.

Although sweetclover died out within a few years after planting, its initial influence made it worth including in new seedings. Smooth brome and intermediate wheatgrass also are recommended in mixture plantings, even though neither species held up well individually under any of the grazing intensities studied. However, both species provided good daily gains, per-acre gains, and high grazing capacities in the early years of treatment which justified their inclusion in mixture plantings. Daily gains decreased as they died out, but overall yields of forage and beef were greater than on crested wheatgrass seeded in pure stands.

Grazing of mixture ranges can begin in the spring when maximum leaf lengths average approximately 4 inches on the crested wheatgrass plants. These ranges should then be stocked heavily enough to

Table 3.—Weight gain of yearling cattle from seeded ranges that are best adapted to the ponderosa pine type (from Currie and Smith 1970).

Year	Seasonal per-acre weight gains				
	Crested wheatgrass	Smooth brome	Mixture	Intermediate wheatgrass	Russian wildrye
	Pounds				
1948	82.2	75.4	85.5	—	—
1949	98.3	83.7	126.3	—	—
1950	50.0	35.0	60.1	83.7	—
1951	44.1	35.7	48.7	43.3	38.0
1952	76.3	62.1	77.8	64.8	51.6
1953	56.8	48.0	68.2	63.6	53.8
1954	10.3	2.8	12.8	12.0	10.3
1955	64.5	38.5	86.3	64.4	82.0
1956	54.0	33.2	65.6	58.6	65.6
1957	79.7	37.2	99.8	57.8	67.3
1958	42.0	18.0	65.6	43.7	28.6
1959	52.7	13.4	62.4	31.0	42.4
Average	59.2	40.2	71.6	52.3	48.8

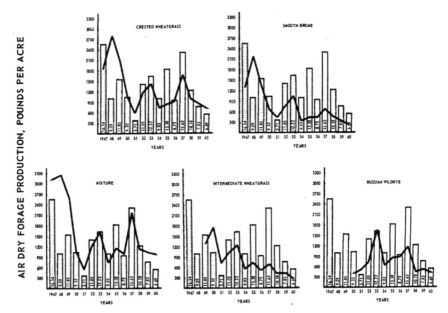

Figure 17.—Pounds per acre of herbage produced by seeded species in relation to the amount of growing-season precipitation (from Currie and Smith 1970).

15

make uniform use of the available forage. Grazing to a 2-inch stubble height, or approximately 65 percent use of the forage by weight, is recommended. Springfield (1963) made similar recommendations for grazing crested wheatgrass in northern New Mexico: start spring grazing when plants are 4 to 5 inches tall, and take animals off the range when utilization averages 65 to 70 percent.

Ground cover, particularly litter, may be reduced with these heavy rates of utilization, but invasion by undesirable species will not be much greater than from grazing at lighter intensities. The advantages of a good level of forage production, more uniform utilization, and greater animal gains per acre, make grazing to a 2-inch stubble height preferable to grazing at a lighter rate unless the additional cover is needed for erosion control and watershed protection purposes.

Russian wildrye, seeded in pure stands, started growth an average of about 3 weeks earlier than other seeded species. Thus where early spring forage is advantageous, this species will provide forage before other seeded species are ready for use. Grazing to approximately a 3-inch stubble height is recommended for Russian wildrye, which should avoid development of ungrazed wolf plants and eventual overgrazed local areas. It should be realized, however, that animal weight gains will usually be smaller than those from ranges seeded to a mixture. Also, Hervey and Johnson (1954) found that Russian wildrye does not fill in between rows following establishment, and concluded that this characteristic may be a disadvantage in high wind or water erosion areas.

Sherman big bluegrass, which was tested later than the other species (Currie 1969a), produced daily gains comparable to crested wheatgrass but less than for intermediate wheatgrass or the mixture. In terms of total beef production and grazing capacity, however, it was superior to any of the other species. Beef production on Sherman big bluegrass averaged 6.7 pounds per acre more than on the mixture, and 19.1 pounds per acre more than on crested wheatgrass. It produced from 54 to 200 pounds more forage per acre, respectively, than these ranges when grazed to a proper 4-inch stubble height. In addition, this species started growth as early as Russian wildrye, and was more drought-tolerant than any of the other species tested.

Crested wheatgrass, which receives the most widespread use in range seedings, was tested to determine which season of use was best for sustained livestock and herbage production (Currie 1970). Grazing this species to a 1-inch stubble height for 10 years during spring only, fall only, or spring and fall, had little effect on the vegetation. Drought and growing-season moisture had more influence on these ranges than the season of grazing. Pastures grazed in spring and fall produced more forage and gave the highest average beef yields, 177 pounds of gain per season.

A method of stepwise regression analysis was developed for estimating forage yields of crested wheatgrass ranges by measuring the monthly precipitation received during the growing season (Currie and Peterson 1966). Precipitation accounted for 88 to 97 percent of the differences in yields, and the amounts received during different months or combinations of months determined the effective forage production available for use by livestock at each season. Precipitation received in April primarily determined forage yields on ranges grazed only in the spring. For ranges grazed only in the fall, May-July rainfall was most useful for predicting yields. When ranges were grazed both spring and fall, April-May precipitation determined spring yields and June-July rainfall controlled fall forage production. Stocking rates in relation to forage yields during the different grazing seasons were also determined. Correlation coefficients between stocking rates (y) and effective forage production at each season (x) ranged from 0.94 for spring grazing on spring-fall ranges to 0.99 for ranges grazed only in the fall (fig. 18). The methods of analyses used should be applicable to determining production and stocking rates on many western rangelands, and should also serve as a means of accounting for variation in certain types of research studies.

Cultural Manipulation and Integrated Systems of Management

Cultural Practices

In addition to range seeding, other cultural practices such as herbicide spraying and range fertilization can be used to improve ranges and increase grazing capacities. Abandoned fields (Johnson 1945) or severely depleted ranges (Costello and Schwan 1946) are most responsive to these kinds of treatment. Principal plants which characterize these stands, and will maintain themselves with grazing, are: fringed sagebrush, tumblegrass, trailing fleabane, and hairy goldaster. The more valuable bunchgrasses — Arizona fescue, mountain muhly, and pine dropseed — are present only in scattered or small fragmented clumps. On granitic soils in the pine-bunchgrass type, these species generally responded to applications of a complete nitrogen-phosphorus-potassium (NPK) fertilizer (Retzer

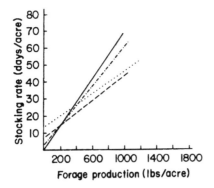

Figure 18.—Stocking rates for crested wheatgrass in relation to forage production and season of grazing (adapted from Currie and Peterson 1966).

Stocking = yearling helfers

Spring plus fall
——————— Spring
- - - - - - Fall

Once each year
—·—··—·— Spring
··············· Fall

(1954). Recent investigations[5] have shown that 50 pounds of elemental material of each fertilizer. produces excellent response, and will increase total herbage yields an average of about 500 pounds per acre (including the less desirable species). The more desirable bunchgrasses can be improved by spraying these depleted areas with 2.5 pounds acid equivalent of 2-4 dichlorophenoxyacetic acid (2,4-D). Spraying should be done early in the spring as the temperature in the top several inches of soil reaches or exceeds 50°F. Application of a complete fertilizer in combination with the herbicide treatment enhances growth of the residual grass plants. Fertilization increased herbage yields from native ranges about 500 pounds per acre. Fertilizing plus spraying increased yields about the same amount, but the herbage was mostly desirable grasses not affected by the herbicide:

	1968	1969	1970	1971	Average
Fertilized	2,110	1,778	1,477	686	1,513
Sprayed	690	1,151	1,407	646	973
Fertilized and sprayed	1,627	1,965	1,595	765	1,488
Control	1,044	1,099	1,148	546	959

Fertilization was also used on Sherman big bluegrass to modify the root growth of this species and reduce the ease with which it is pulled up by grazing cattle. Nitrogen or phosphorus alone reduced the tensions required to pull the plants, but N and P together made pulling more difficult than for control plants receiving no fertilizer treatment (fig. 19). Evaluation of plant root systems and top growth in

[5]Currie, Pat O. Recovery of ponderosa pine-bunchgrass ranges through grazing and herbicide or fertilizer treatments. (Manuscript in preparation at Rocky Mt. For. and Range Exp. Stn., Fort Collins, Colo.)

glass-faced planter boxes indicated a close correlation between the total root system weight and the tension required to pull the plants (Haferkamp and Currie 1973).

Integrating Native — Seeded Ranges

Length of the grazing season in which animals make good gains can be substantially increased by including seeded ranges in a management system with native ranges (Currie 1966, 1969b). Average weaning weights of calves grazed on the combination seeded-native range system of management (fig. 20) were consistently heavier than those grazed on native range only:

	Weaning weights on --	
	Seeded-native	Native
Year	range	range
	(Pounds)	
1963	439	422
1964	416	389
1965	462	446
1966	465	420
Average	446	419

For this study, two herds of 12 cows each followed the same grazing system for a 10-year comparison period.

Although most of the weight gain advantage came from fall grazing of Sherman big bluegrass, the Russian wildrye and crested wheatgrass contributed significantly to long-term animal nutrition. Malechek (1966) found that crude protein (fig. 21) was sufficient to excessive for 10 months in the diets of

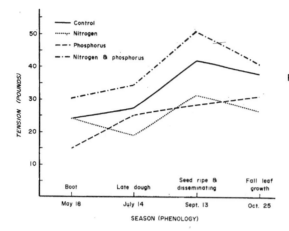

Figure 19.—The tension required for grazing livestock to pull up or break Sherman big bluegrass plants can be modified by adding fertilizer. A combination of 50 pounds each of nitrogen and phosphorus most effectively reduced pullup.

fistulated animals when seeded ranges were integrated into the management system, compared to only 8 months for animals grazing only native forage plants. Earlier growth and later dormancy of the seeded species was largely responsible for the nutritional difference.

Dormant-season grazing of Sherman big bluegrass during November through March minimized the pullup problem of this species, and also produced satisfactory overwinter weight gains (Currie 1975). Big bluegrass usually provided abundant forage for overwintering weaner heifer calves. The animals gained weight in late fall with or without a protein supplement. Weight losses during winter and spring were relatively small, usually averaging less than 20 pounds per animal. Feeding a protein supplement to prevent or reduce such a small weight loss probably is not justified. In addition, big bluegrass supported two to three times more animals than a comparable acreage of native range, and when supplemented with ¼ or ½ pound of protein produced nearly twice as many pounds of beef per acre as did native range.

Additional Practices

Several universally recognized range management practices are applicable for improving livestock dis-

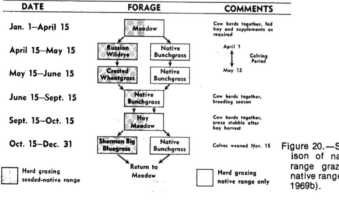

Figure 20.—Schematic comparison of native plus seeded range grazing system with native range only (from Currie 1969b).

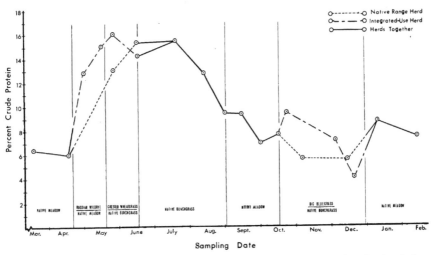

Figure 21.—Annual trends of dietary crude protein in forage samples collected by fistulated steers (from Malechek 1966).

tribution, encouraging the most efficient stocking rates, and obtaining more uniform use of the forage on ponderosa pine-bunchgrass ranges (Skovlin 1965). These practices include: Fencing for better livestock control and distribution, development or hauling of water, adjusting salt grounds to encourage uniform use, range riding, and construction of trails and driveways to move livestock and improve access. One or more of these practices would be appropriate for nearly all ranges. There is no one standard prescription, however; problems must be resolved for each specific range unit, but attention to one or more of these practices can determine the success or failure of the more complex procedures.

Factors Affecting the Future of Livestock Grazing and Range Research

Land Use Patterns and Priorities

In evaluating grazing and other problems of the ponderosa pine type, it is essential that we objectively review current and expected land use priorities. Earlier land use problems revolved around such activities as mining, developing access roads and railroads, obtaining adequate timber for construction and fuel, and growing crops to sustain the expanding population. The important grazing problem of those

times was locating ranges with the most prolific vegetation, and converting forage into a maximum of beef as quickly, profitably, and close to consumer markets as possible. These uses of the ponderosa pine-bunchgrass type have decreased while other uses have increased in importance. Not enough is known of the impacts of one use upon another — which are compatible, which are not. Future research in the pine country must therefore include multiple uses, to determine how and where grazing fits into the land use pattern.

Most cattle that graze on the National Forest lands of Colorado utilize ponderosa pine-bunchgrass ranges, at least part of the season. Therefore, the following data are closely related to the pine-bunchgrass type: In 1956, 152,887 cattle grazed on Colorado's National Forests, about half the 306,656 that grazed in 1940. Animal months dropped even more — 57.5 percent. Permittees numbered 3,506 in 1940 and 1,847 in 1956, a decrease of about 47 percent. Since 1956, animal numbers have stayed almost the same, but the number of permittees has declined another 25 percent.

Some 30 percent of ponderosa pine bunchgrass ranges, within and adjacent to National Forests of the Front Range, are privately owned. Such land is usually located along streams and on other productive sites. Amount of grazing provided by these holdings is unknown, but the amount of forage

19

produced is undoubtedly as large as that produced on public lands. It appears likely that these private rangelands, occupying the most fertile sites, will continue to be of great importance, but often for uses other than grazing.

Water has been and will continue to be a primary resource in regulating land use activities. Water yield from the ponderosa pine-bunchgrass ranges amounts to 3 to 5 inches annually, about 20 percent of the annual precipitation, or 4 million acre-feet. In contrast, water yield from the higher Continental Divide area amounts to 12 to 18 inches, or about 50 to 70 percent of the annual precipitation. This difference is primarily due to the overwinter snow accumulation before melt starts at the higher elevations. Only on the north exposures does snow accumulate in the ponderosa pine-bunchgrass ranges. On south exposures and in the valley bottoms, winter snows melt soon after a storm.

In 1950, a Forest Service report prepared for the President's Water Resources Policy Commission (USDA FS 1950), in discussing problems in the Missouri River Basin, made these interesting statements: "A major use of water . . . is for irrigation . . . A secondary, but essential use . . . is for livestock . . . The generation of hydro-electric power is becoming a very important use . . . Another important use of water which has not been fully recognized is for recreation . . . the use of water for industrial purposes is rather limited (but) use . . . for this purpose will increase . . . The primary function of these lands . . . is to regulate streamflow and to prevent sedimentation. Most of these lands may be used also for timber production, grazing, and recreation in varying degrees without adversely affecting their watershed protective values."

Recreation, including hunting and fishing, has become the second most important use of National Forests in the upper Arkansas and South Platte watersheds (Reid and Love 1951). In the Rocky Mountain Region (R-2) of the Forest Service, recreational visits increased from slightly over 2 million in 1946, to over 16 million in 1970. Ponderosa pine country flanking the eastern slopes of the central Rockies bore the brunt of this accelerated use, as people from population centers from Laramie to Albuquerque "have gone to the mountains" for recreation.

Complementary to recreation use has been the development of homes in ponderosa pine country. Once classed as summer homes, it was estimated in 1953 that some 800 such homes had been constructed on the public lands of the pine type. Since that time, thousands of homes have been developed on private lands within the type, but they are now usually yearlong residences of people commuting to urban centers. In their leisure time, and as a result of building roads, cutting trees, using water, and other activities, these residents exert a considerable impact on the natural resources. In addition, ponderosa pine lands which were once operational livestock ranches have been sold as real estate developments. Thus, grazing continues to decrease in the pine type.

Estimates of future requirements for wood products indicate it may become necessary to harvest low-quality second-growth timber. Following World War II, harvesting of timber in the ponderosa pine-bunchgrass type steadily declined. Spruce, fir, and lodgepole pine replaced the ponderosa pine because of its lowered quality and small size. Yet, about 9.5 billion board-feet of timber is available in the pine country; most of it in the form of second-growth trees. Associated with anticipated use of ponderosa pine timber is the demand for Christmas trees. Harvesting these small trees is a useful means of improving the growth of pine and its companion, Douglas-fir.

Relating Demands to Resource Capabilities

The important consideration is that total demands upon a constant or diminishing forest resource base continue to mount. Intelligent appraisals of resources and demands will be required to adequately meet the challenge. The primary objective of future natural resource research in the ponderosa pine-bunchgrass type should be to obtain direct solutions to fundamental aspects of problems. The relationship of timber harvest and grazing, for example, to trout production in streams, to production of forage for deer and elk, and to picnicking and camping activities are important questions. More complete knowledge of such relationships will make possible the development and adoption of sound land use practices to derive the maximum total value from grazing, water yield, timber production, and recreational opportunity.

To meet these objectives, more general knowledge of the ponderosa pine-bunchgrass ranges is needed. We need to know the amount and location of merchantable timber and usable grazing lands, the distribution of soil types and their productive and hydrologic characteristics, streamflow and weather characteristics for drainages originating in the pine type, and the motivation, use areas, and demands that campers, picnickers, hunters, and fishermen place on the forest, range, and water resources. This knowledge should encompass the common range of exposures, slopes, soils, and vegetation subtypes found within the pine country.

Literature Cited

Alexander, Robert R.
1974. Silviculture of subalpine forests in the central and southern Rocky Mountains: The status of our knowledge. USDA For. Serv. Res. Pap. RM-121, 88 p. Rocky Mt. For. and Range Exp. Stn., Fort Collins, Colo.

Chronic, John, and Halka Chronic.
1972. Prairie, peak, and plateau — a guide to the geology of Colorado. Colo. Geol. Surv. Bull. 32, 126 p. Colo. Geol. Surv., Denver, Colo.

Costello, David F., and H. E. Schwan.
1946. Conditions and trends on ponderosa pine ranges in Colorado. U.S. For. Serv., Rocky Mt. For. and Range Exp. Stn., 33 p. [mimeo].

Currie, Pat O.
1966. Seeded range improves calf weaning weights and profits. Colo. Rancher Farmer 20(6):5.

Currie, Pat O.
1967. Seeding Sherman big bluegrass. J. Range Manage. 20:133-136.

Currie, Pat O.
1969a. Plant response and cattle gains on Sherman big bluegrass. J. Range Manage. 22:258-261.

Currie, Pat O.
1969b. Use seeded ranges in your management. J. Range Manage. 22:432-434.

Currie, Pat O.
1970. Influence of spring, fall and spring-fall grazing on crested wheatgrass range. J. Range Manage. 23:103-108.

Currie, Pat O.
1975. Plant response and livestock weight changes on big bluegrass range grazed during late fall, winter, and early spring. J. Range Manage. 28:340-343.

Currie, Pat O., and Geraldine Peterson.
1966. Using growing-season precipitation to predict crested wheatgrass yields. J. Range Manage. 19:284-288.

Currie, Pat O., and Dwight R. Smith.
1970. Response of seeded ranges to different grazing intensities in the ponderosa pine zone of Colorado. U.S. Dep. Agric., Prod. Res. Rep. 112, 41 p.

Dortignac, E. J., and L. D. Love.
1960. Relation of plant cover to infiltration and erosion in ponderosa pine forests in Colorado. Am. Soc. Agric. Eng. Trans. 3:58-61.

Dortignac, E. J., and L. D. Love.
1961. Infiltration studies on ponderosa pine ranges of Colorado. U.S. Dep. Agric., For. Serv., Rocky Mt. For. and Range Exp. Stn., Stn. Pap. 59, 34 p. Fort Collins, Colo.

Dunford, E. G.
1954. Surface runoff and erosion from pine grasslands of the Colorado Front Range. J. For. 52:923-927.

Gary, Howard L.
1975. Watershed management problems and opportunities for the Colorado Front Range ponderosa pine zone: The status of our knowledge. USDA For. Serv. Res. Pap. RM-139, 32 p. Rocky Mt. For. and Range Exp. Stn., Fort Collins, Colo.

Haferkamp, M. R., and P. O. Currie.
1973. Effects of fertilizer on root strength of Sherman big bluegrass (Poa ampla Merr.) Agron. J. 65:511-512.

Hervey, D. F., and W. M. Johnson.
1954. Don't overlook Russian wild rye. Colo. Farm Home Res. 5(4):3, 4, 11.

Hull, A. C., Jr., and W. M. Johnson.
1955. Range seeding in the ponderosa pine zone of Colo. U.S. Dep. Agric., Circ. 953, 40 p.

Johnson, W. M.
1945. Natural revegetation of abandoned crop land in the ponderosa pine zone of the Pike's Peak region in Colorado. Ecology 26:363-374.

Johnson, W. M.
1947. Return of abandoned fields to forage production can be hastened by reseeding. Colo. A&M News 1(12):6.

Johnson, W. M.
1953. Effect of grazing intensity upon vegetation and cattle gains on ponderosa pine-bunchgrass ranges of the Front Range of Colorado. U.S. Dep. Agric., Circ. 929, 36 p.

Johnson, W. M.
1959. Grazing intensity trials on seeded ranges in the ponderosa pine zone of Colorado. J. Range Manage. 12:1-7.

Johnson, W. M., and A. C. Hull, Jr.
1950. How to reseed parks and openings in the ponderosa pine zone in Colorado. U.S. Dep. Agric., For. Serv., Rocky Mt. For. and Range Exp. Stn., Stn. Pap. 3, 14 p. Fort Collins, Colo.

Johnson, W. M., and Elbert H. Reid.
1958. Herbage utilization on pine-bunchgrass ranges of Colorado. J. For. 56:647-651.

Love, L. D.
1953. Watershed management experiments in the Colorado Front Range. J. Soil Water Conserv. 8:213-218.

Love, L. D.
1958. Rangeland watershed management. Soc. Am. For. [Salt Lake City, Utah, Sept.-Oct. 1958] Proc. 1958:198-200.

Malechek, John C.
1966. Cattle diets on native and seeded ranges in the ponderosa pine zone of Colorado. U.S. For. Serv. Res. Note RM-77, 12 p. Rocky Mt. For. and Range Exp. Stn., Fort Collins, Colo.

Marcus, Steven R.
1973. Geology of the Montane Zone of central Colorado — with emphasis on Manitou Park. USDA For. Serv. Res. Pap. RM-113, 20 p. Rocky Mt. For. and Range Exp. Stn., Fort Collins, Colo.

McGinnies, W. J., D. F. Hervey, J. A. Downs, and A. C. Everson.
1963. A summary of range grass seeding trials in Colorado. Colo. Agric. Exp. Stn., Tech. Bull. 73, 81 p.

Miller, Robert L., and Grover A. Choate.
1964. The forest resource of Colorado. U.S. For. Serv. Resour. Bull. INT-3, 55 p. Intermt. For. and Range Exp. Stn., Ogden, Utah.

Reid, Elbert H., and L. D. Love.
1951. Range-watershed conditions and recommendations for management, Elk Ridge and Lower Elk Ridge cattle allotments, Roosevelt National Forest, Colorado. 123 p. U.S. Dep. Agric., For. Serv., Wash., D.C.

Reifsnyder, William E., and Howard W. Lull.
1965. Radiant energy in relation to forests. U.S. Dep. Agric., Tech. Bull. 1344, 111 p.

Renner, F. G., and L. D. Love.
1955. Management of water and western rangelands. U.S. Dep. Agric. Yearb. 1955:415-423.

Retzer, J. L.
1954. Fertilization of some range soils in the Rocky Mountains. J. Range Manage. 7:69-73.

Schuster, Joseph L.
1964. Root development of native plants under three grazing intensities. Ecology 45:63-70.

Skovlin, Jon M.
1965. Improving cattle distribution on western mountain rangelands. U.S. Dep. Agric., Farmers Bull. 2212, 14 p.

Smith, Dwight R.
1967. Effects of cattle grazing on a ponderosa pine-bunchgrass range in Colorado. U.S. Dep. Agric., Tech. Bull. 1371, 60 p.

Springfield, H. W.
1963. Cattle gains and plant responses from spring grazing on crested wheatgrass in northern New Mexico. U.S. Dep. Agric., Prod. Res. Rep. 74, 46 p.

U.S. Department of Agriculture, Forest Service.
1950. Forests and water in the Missouri River Basin, 42 p. [Rep. prepared for President's Water Resour. Policy Comm., Wash., D.C.]

lants

Grasses and Grasslike

luegrass, Sherman big	*Poa ampla* Merr.
luestem, little	*Andropogon scoparius* Michx.
rome, smooth	*Bromus inermis* Leyss.
)ropseed, pine	*Blepharoneuron tricho-lepis* (Torr.) Nash
'escue, Arizona	*Festuca arizonica* Vasey
'escue, Idaho	*Festuca idahoensis* Elmer
'escue, sheep	*Festuca ovina* L.
'escue, Thurber	*Festuca thurberii* Vasey
3rama, blue	*Bouteloua gracilis* (H.B.K.) Lag.
Hairgrasses	*Deschampsia* spp.
'unegrass	*Koeleria cristata* (L.) Pers.
Muhly, mountain	*Muhlenbergia montana* (Nutt.) Hitchc.
Muhly, pullup	*Muhlenbergia filiformis* (Thurb.) Rydb.
Muhly, screwleaf	*Muhlenbergia virescens* (H.B.K.) Kunth.
Oatgrass, Parry	*Danthonia parryi* Scribn.
Rushes	*Juncus* spp.
Sedges	*Carex* spp.
Sedge, sun	*Carex heliophila* Mackenz.
Sleepygrass	*Stipa robusta* (Vasey) Scribn.
Squirreltail, bottlebrush	*Sitanion hystrix* (Nutt.) J. G. Smith
Tumblegrass	*Schedonnardus panicula-tus* (Nutt.) Trel.
Wheatgrass, crested	*Agropyron cristatum* (L.) Gaertn.
Wheatgrass, intermediate	*Agropyron intermedium* (Host) Beauv.
Wheatgrass, slender	*Agropyron trachycaulum* (Link) Malte
Wheatgrass, western	*Agropyron smithii* Rydb.
Wildrye, Russian	*Elymus junceus* Fisch.

Forbs

Asters	*Aster* spp.
Bluebells	*Mertensia* spp.
Cinquefoils	*Potentilla* spp.
Fleabane, trailing	*Erigeron flagellaris* A. Gray
Geranium, Fremont	*Geranium fremonti* Torr.
Geranium, Parry	*Geranium parryi* Engelm.
Goldaster, hairy	*Chrysopsis villosa* (Pursh.) Nutt.
Goosefoot	*Chenopodium album* L.
Groundsel	*Senecio fendleri* Gray
Loco, Lambert	*Oxytropis lambertii* Pursh
Lupines	*Lupinus* spp.
Milkvetch, purple	*Astragalus striatus* Nutt.
Pussytoes, Rocky Mountain	*Antennaria parvifolia* Nutt.
Sagebrush, fringed	*Artemisia frigida* Willd.
Sweetclover, yellow-blossom	*Melilotus officinalis* (L.) Lam.
Yarrow, western	*Achillea lanulosa* Nutt.

Trees and Shrubs

Aspen, quaking	*Populus tremuloides* Michx.
Bearberry	*Arctostaphylos uva-ursi* (L.) Spreng.
Cinquefoil, shrubby	*Potentilla fruticosa* L.
Douglas-fir, Rocky Mountain	*Pseudotsuga menziesii* var. *glauca* (Beissn.) Franco.
Fir, subalpine	*Abies lasiocarpa* (Hook.) Nutt.
Oak brush	*Quercus* spp.
Pine, lodgepole	*Pinus contorta* Dougl.
Pine, ponderosa	*Pinus ponderosa* Lawson
Rose, Arkansas	*Rosa arkansana* Porter
Spruce, Engelmann	*Picea engelmannii* Parry
Willows	*Salix* spp.

23

Mammals

A list compiled for the Manitou Experimental Forest[6] is representative for the Eastern Slope pine type. The abbreviated list below includes the common large and small mammals. The Western Slope pine type would have many of the same genera and some of the same species. A few additional animals such as the elk (*Cervus canadensis* Erxleben) in western Colorado and the ring-tailed cat (*Bassariscus astutus* Lichtenstein) in New Mexico would be other more common species to be included.

Lagomorpha

Cottontail, mountain	*Sylvilagus nuttalli*
Jackrabbit, white-tailed	*Lepus townsendi*

Carnivora

Bear, black	*Ursus americanus*
Bobcat	*Lynx rufus*
Coyote	*Canus latrans*
Fox, red	*Vulpes fulva*
Mink	*Mustela vison*
Weasel, long-tailed	*Mustela frenata*

[6]List prepared by Vincent H. Reid, Wildlife Biologist, Res. Bur. Sport Fish. and Wildl., USDI Fish and Wildl. Serv., Fort Collins, Colo.

Artiodactyla

Deer, mule	*Odocoileus hemionus*

Insectivora

Shrew, masked	*Sorex cinereus*
Shrew, vagrant	*Sorex vagrans*

Rodentia

Beaver	*Castor canadensis*
Chipmunk, Colorado	*Eutamias quadrivittatus*
Chipmunk, least	*Eutamias minimus*
Gopher, northern pocket	*Thomomys talpoides*
Ground squirrel, golden-mantled	*Spermothilus lateralis*
Ground squirrel, thirteen-lined	*Spermothilus tridecemlineatus*
Marmot, yellow-bellied	*Marmota flaviventris*
Mouse, deer	*Peromyscus maniculatus*
Mouse, western jumping	*Zapus princeps*
Muskrat	*Ondatra zibethicus*
Porcupine	*Erethizon dorsatum*
Prairie dog, white-tailed	*Cynomys gunnisoni*
Squirrel, red	*Tamiasciurus hudsonicus*
Squirrel, tassel-eared	*Sciurus aberti*
Vole, meadow	*Microtus pennsylvanicus*
Vole, long-tailed	*Microtus longicaudus*

Currie, Pat O.
1975. Grazing management of ponderosa pine-bunchgrass ranges of the central Rocky Mountains: The status of our knowledge. USDA For. Serv. Res. Pap. RM-159, 24 p. Rocky Mt. For. and Range Exp. Stn., Fort Collins, Colo. 80521

Pine-bunchgrass ranges have historically been important livestock-producing areas in the central Rocky Mountains. Grazing will continue to be important, but in conjunction with other uses of the land. Livestock-management techniques are well developed and soundly based on research within the pine-bunchgrass type. There is a need, however, to understand the interrelationships of other land uses, particularly as they relate to human population pressures. Research needs, as well as what is known, are described for several vegetation cover types. Other resources, such as timber, soil, and water, are evaluated in relation to grazing.
Keywords: Grazing management, pine-bunchgrass type, *Pinus ponderosa.*

Currie, Pat O.
1975. Grazing management of ponderosa pine-bunchgrass ranges of the central Rocky Mountains: The status of our knowledge. USDA For. Serv. Res. Pap. RM-159, 24 p. Rocky Mt. For. and Range Exp. Stn., Fort Collins, Colo. 80521

Pine-bunchgrass ranges have historically been important livestock-producing areas in the central Rocky Mountains. Grazing will continue to be important, but in conjunction with other uses of the land. Livestock-management techniques are well developed and soundly based on research within the pine-bunchgrass type. There is a need, however, to understand the interrelationships of other land uses, particularly as they relate to human population pressures. Research needs, as well as what is known, are described for several vegetation cover types. Other resources, such as timber, soil, and water, are evaluated in relation to grazing.
Keywords: Grazing management, pine-bunchgrass type, *Pinus ponderosa.*

Currie, Pat O.
1975. Grazing management of ponderosa pine-bunchgrass ranges of the central Rocky Mountains: The status of our knowledge. USDA For. Serv. Res. Pap. RM-159, 24 p. Rocky Mt. For. and Range Exp. Stn., Fort Collins, Colo. 80521

Pine-bunchgrass ranges have historically been important livestock-producing areas in the central Rocky Mountains. Grazing will continue to be important, but in conjunction with other uses of the land. Livestock-management techniques are well developed and soundly based on research within the pine-bunchgrass type. There is a need, however, to understand the interrelationships of other land uses, particularly as they relate to human population pressures. Research needs, as well as what is known, are described for several vegetation cover types. Other resources, such as timber, soil, and water, are evaluated in relation to grazing.
Keywords: Grazing management, pine-bunchgrass type, *Pinus ponderosa.*

Currie, Pat O.
1975. Grazing management of ponderosa pine-bunchgrass ranges of the central Rocky Mountains: The status of our knowledge. USDA For. Serv. Res. Pap. RM-159, 24 p. Rocky Mt. For. and Range Exp. Stn., Fort Collins, Colo. 80521

Pine-bunchgrass ranges have historically been important livestock-producing areas in the central Rocky Mountains. Grazing will continue to be important, but in conjunction with other uses of the land. Livestock-management techniques are well developed and soundly based on research within the pine-bunchgrass type. There is a need, however, to understand the interrelationships of other land uses, particularly as they relate to human population pressures. Research needs, as well as what is known, are described for several vegetation cover types. Other resources, such as timber, soil, and water, are evaluated in relation to grazing.
Keywords: Grazing management, pine-bunchgrass type, *Pinus ponderosa.*

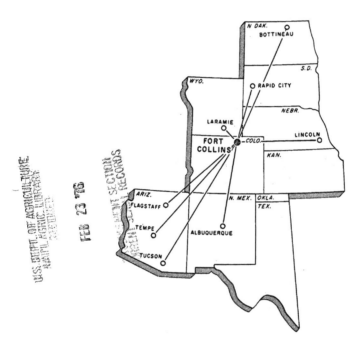